Flavors of
Mexico

Flavors of
Mexico

Clare Ferguson

photography by **Jeremy Hopley**

AN IMPRINT OF RUNNING PRESS
PHILADELPHIA • LONDON

Designer **Megan Smith**

Design Assistant **Stuart Edwards**

Editor **Elsa Petersen-Schepelern**

Creative Director **Jacqui Small**

Publishing Director **Anne Ryland**

Production **Meryl Silbert**

Food Stylist **Clare Ferguson**

Stylist **Wei Tang**

Photographer's Assistant **Catherine Rowlands**

Indexer **Hilary Bird**

Author Photograph **Graeme Harris**

Dedication
To my husband, Ian Ferguson, for his encouragement.

Acknowledgements
My thanks to the A team; Jeremy Hopley, Wei Tang, Catherine Rowlands, Nicky
Rogerson, Karl Rixon, Megan Smith, Elsa Petersen-Schepelern, and Fiona
Smith. Thanks also to Christopher Robbins and Christine Boodle for technical
advice, Dodie Miller of The Cool Chile Company for her advice on dried chiles
and other Mexican products, Birgit Erath of The Spice Shop, Sarah Wain of
West Dean Gardens for her fresh chiles, and Teresa Cervera and Amelia Garcia
Leigh for their help with the translations. Thanks also to my suppliers; butchers
David Lidgate and Kingsland, and greengrocers the Michanicou Brothers and
Hyams & Cockerton. Thanks to La Mexicana Quality Foods for the tortillas. My
appreciation also to my agents Fiona Lindsay and Linda Shanks.

Notes
All spoon measurements are level unless otherwise specified.
Ovens should be preheated to the specified temperature. If using
a convection oven, adjust times and temperature according to the
manufacturer's instructions.

Produced by Toppan, Hong Kong
Printed and bound in China

10 9 8 7 6 5 4 3 2 1

Library of Congress Cataloging-in-Publication number
97-77957

ISBN 0-7624-0359-4

This edition published in the United States of America in 1998 by
Courage Books, an imprint of
Running Press Book Publishers
125 South Twenty-second Street
Philadelphia, Pennsylvania 19103-4399

contents

introduction

Mexico has always been a country of passionate contrasts and its cooking reflects its turbulent history, richness, and excitement. The meeting of the Old World and the New created dishes that are colorful, delicious, and diverse. Though sophisticated agricultural systems flourished in Mexico from pre-history, when the Spanish arrived they created profound change. Equally, the Old World gained, along with the territory, culinary treasures galore.

Before 1492, when Columbus made landfall in the Americas, many now-familiar foods were unknown. Think of the world without turkey, corn, tomatoes, sweet peppers, chiles, dozens of different beans, or squash such as zucchinis and pumpkin. These, together with peanuts, avocados, guavas, pineapples, chocolate, and vanilla are just some of the gifts Mexico bestowed on an astonished world.

Mexico boasts one of the world's great cuisines, with the three facets of society—peasants, priests, and princes—contributing to the changes which elevated the Mexican kitchen tradition to its zenith.

Today Mexican food means more than tacos, tamales, and tongue-scorching salsas. We are discovering the convivial pleasures of quickly prepared *antojitos* and *entremeses*, seafood with elegant recados, roasted, broiled, or barbecued poultry and meats with clean, spicy adobos and salsas. Tortillas—versatile, easy, and fun—come in hundreds of different guises. Beans, too, are an unlimited resource, for Mexicans elevate *frijoles* to a high art. Mountains of vivid vegetables, herbs, and grains, ancient and modern, enliven the diet. Salads are fresh and stylish. Chiles, fresh and dried, add their fruity, spicy warmth to many, but not most dishes. Fruity puddings, sticky cakes, fine pastries, silky custards are undeniable treats.

I hope my recipes and these pictures will fire you with a new enthusiasm for the glorious flavors of Mexico. *Buen provecho!*

Mexican ingredients

The Americas, especially Mexico, contributed countless new foodstuffs to the global larder after Columbus's world-changing voyage in 1492. Imagine, for instance, life without potatoes, corn, and tomatoes. Conversely, traditional ingredients from the Old World were taken to the Americas, so that items like plantains, bananas, and cheese are now integral parts of New World cuisines.

HERBS

1. Common herbs include, from left:

Parsley the continental, Italian, or flat-leaf parsley is used in Mexico.

Cilantro, or Chinese parsley, is widely used.

Oregano and Marjoram Use either Mexican or common varieties. Pan-toast before use.

Thyme is used fresh and dry, especially in cooking meat, broths, sauces, and pickles.

Bay leaf ordinary bay leaves can be substituted for Mexican bay.

Mexican herbs (not shown) include:

Epazote (goosefoot, wormseed, or Mexican tea) has a scent of camphor and is best used fresh. It grows wild and is easy to cultivate. The most classic of Mexican herbs, it is seen as essential for beans. There is no substitute.

Hierba santa/Hoja santa has heart-shaped leaves used for flavoring or wrapping. There is no substitute. In this book, I have used other herbs, though they give a different flavor.

Hierbabuena/Yerba buena is spearmint. Other mints may be used if this is unobtainable.

FRUITS AND VEGETABLES

Favorite Mexican fruits and vegetables, both indigenous and imported, include:

2. Avocado is native to Mexico. From left:

Haas with dark knobbly skin, is the variety with the best flavor.

Fuerte with smooth skin has a bland taste.

Reed is very large with hard shell-like skin, large stone, and bland taste. Always use avocado fresh or add to a dish at the end of cooking—when heated it becomes bitter.

3

8

5

7

3. Plantain is a large, thick-skinned, cooking banana, never eaten raw. Like the rest of the banana family, it is native to India, and was introduced to the Americas via West Africa. It ripens from green to yellow and then black. If unobtainable, substitute ordinary bananas, either green or ripe. In Mexico, plantains are mostly used when black and ripe. They taste a little like sweet potatoes. Sold in Caribbean, Asian, and Latin-American stores.

4. Choko or chayote, also known as mirliton or christophene, is a pale green, pear-shaped squash with sweet, succulent flesh. Native to Mexico, it is now widely used in Asia. They are sold in Asian and Caribbean stores, and in larger supermarkets. If unobtainable zucchinis may be substituted.

5. Tomatillo is an acidic, green fruit with a papery husk, related to the physalis or cape gooseberry. The basis of many sauces, it is usually husked, blanched, and chopped before use. It is sometimes found fresh in specialist markets, but is more widely available canned. It is a signature ingredient in Mexican cooking and, although there is no true substitute, unripe tomatoes are often used instead.

6. Cactus fruits, also known as prickly pears or Indian figs, have prickly skins. They are peeled, then eaten in pies, salsas, or salads. They are also eaten fresh, often sprinkled with chile powder. The prickly paddle-shaped cactus leaves or *nopales* (not shown) are peeled and used as a vegetable.

LEAVES

7. Leaves used as wrappers include, from left:
Banana leaf is used to wrap food for cooking and gives a faint flavor. It is also used as a serving surface. Available from Asian and Latin-American stores.
Corn husks are green and pliant when fresh, pale and brittle when dried. Used as tamale-wrappers. Dried husks are soaked and simmered before use.
Avocado leaf (not shown) leaves from the mature tree are wrapped around foods before cooking, and give an aniseed flavor.

CHEESES

8. Mexican cheeses include, from left:
Queso fresco is a dry curd cheese. Feta or muenster may be used instead.
Queso añejo is a dry, crumbly, salty cheese. Monterey Jack may be substituted .
Queso asadero is a melting cheese. Goat cheese or mozzarella may be substituted.

FRESH CHILES

Mexico and South America are the source of all the world's chiles. Those used in Mexico are known for their complex flavors and spicy heat ranging from mild (0) to very hot (10).

1. Anaheim is large, green, ripening to scarlet. Mild, sweeter when ripe. Developed in the United States. 6 ins. Heat scale: 2–3.

2. Rear, from left:
Pimento is green (left), ripens to red (second left). Sweet, aromatic. Used fresh in salsas, or dried as paprika. Developed in the United States and Europe. 4 ins. Heat scale: 1.
Atorodo glossy, pungent. 4 ins. Heat scale: 5.
Poblano large, dark, greenish-purple ripens to red-brown. Never used raw. Smoky, earthy taste when cooked. Very fiery, it must be cored and seeded. Known as ancho and mulato when dried. 5 ins. Heat scale: 3.
Front, from left:
Chilaca dark brown, fresh form of the dried pasilla. Used in mole sauces together with ancho and mulato. 3 ins. Heat scale: 3–5.
New Mexico is one of the most common varieties grown in the United States. Sweet, earthy, clear-flavored. Mid-green, ripening to bright red. Sometimes twisted or knotty in shape. 6–10 ins. Heat scale: 3–5.

3. Scotch Bonnet from the Caribbean coasts and islands. Distinguished by its convoluted shapes. Green, ripening to a bright, clear yellow or red, with a clear, fruity flavor. One of the hottest chiles. 2 ins. Heat scale: 9.

4. Cayenne and Guajillo green, red when ripe, very hot. This variety is the forefather of Asian chiles. Guajillo, popular in Mexico, is a variety of cayenne. 2 ins. Heat scale: 8.

5. Some of the most widely available chiles include, from top:
Jalapeño well-known and versatile, mostly used when bright green, but ripens to red. Also sold pickled. 2–3 ins. Heat scale: 5.5.
Fresno bright green (left), ripening to bright red (right), with rounded shoulders tapering to a fat, rounded end. Waxy, fleshy, with sweetly hot taste. 1–2 ins. Heat scale: 6.5.
Serrano dark green (right), ripens to scarlet (left). Clean taste with pleasant acidity. Also available pickled. 1–2 ins. Heat scale: 7.

5. Caribbean coastal chiles include, from left:
Güero or Caribe yellow, sweet, used in yellow moles or salsas. 4 ins. Heat scale: 5–7.
Habanero widely used in the Yucatan. Pointy nose distinguishes it from Scotch bonnet and Jamaica hot. Yellow, red, smoky orange or maroon when ripe. 2 ins. Heat scale: 9.
Jamaica Hot distinctive pattypan shape, Mid-green, ripening to scarlet. Fruity and very spicy. 1½ ins. Heat scale: 9.
Not shown: Piquillo roasted, skinned and seeded, used in rajas and stuffings. Often available canned. 4 ins. Heat scale: 2–3.

DRIED CHILES

Mexican dried chiles are known for their sophisticated, smoky flavors. From left:
7. Guajillo is big, glossy, deep orange-red to chestnut in color with sweet, hot taste. Known for its flavor notes of green tea and pine. 4–5 ins. Heat scale: 2–4.
Ancho is the dried form of the poblano (as is the mulato). Dark, brick-red to mahogany with ruby tones. Also available as powder. 4–5 ins. Heat scale: 3–5.
Cascabel is round and fleshy, with rich, smoky, woody flavors. 1 in. Heat scale: 4.

8. Front, from left:
Pasilla or "little raisin"—the dried form of chilaca. Dark, glossy brown with sweet, hot, herb-berry taste. Also used as powder. Poblano and its dried forms, the mulato and ancho, are sometimes wrongly labeled as pasilla. 5–6 ins. Heat scale: 3–5.

New Mexico (Colorado or Dried Californian). Bright scarlet. Earthy flavor with faint dried cherry hints. Often sold as powder or strings (*ristras*). Widely grown in and exported from the United States. 5–7 ins. Heat scale: 2–4.

Choricero is the chile which gave chorizo sausage its name. 3 ins. Heat scale: 5–6

Mulato is dried poblano. Smokier tasting than ancho with hints of cherry and tobacco. Glossy dark chocolate-black. Top grade is sold as *primero* and medium grade as *mediano*. 4–5 ins. Heat scale: 2–4.

Not shown: Chipotle, the smoked, dried jalapeño. Sweet smoky flavor, with subtle, mellow heat. 3–4 ins. Heat scale: 5–6.

CHILE POWDERS AND FLAKES

9. Powders and flakes, from top left:
Paprika from Hungary or Spain. The most widely available chile powder and can be used when hot (top left) or mild (center left) powders from Mexico are unavailable. Dependable quality. Heat scale: 0–4.

Mexican chile powder (top right) ranges from sweet, tangy caribe, to the sweet, mildly hot New Mexico red, and chimayo, from a mountain-grown chile. Heat scale: 3.

Ancho (center right) is made from dried poblanos. Heat scale 3–5.

Crushed chiles Heat scale: varies.

ACHIOTE AND ANNATTO

1. Achiotes are the small, red seeds of the annatto tree, native to South America. They give orange-yellow color and earthy flavor to many Mexican foods. They are also used to color butter, cheese, and smoked fish. The seeds are very hard and, though traditionally ground in a mortar and pestle, most cooks find that an electric spice grinder is an easier, more modern time-saving device. From left, **achiote seeds** (in the jar), **annatto powder** (in the spoon), and **annatto oil** (right).

These seeds are ground to form achiote paste. To make annatto oil, the seeds or powder are infused in an edible oil.

NUTS AND SEEDS

2. Nuts and seeds, both native and exotic, are widely used in Mexican cooking. Clockwise from top left, **pecans, peanuts** (in and out of the shell), and **pumpkin seeds** (*pepitas*). **Walnuts, cashews,** and **sesame seeds** are also widely used. *Pepitas* are common in Mexico as a snack food and thickener.

BEANS

3. Many of the world's beans are native to the Americas. Known as *frijoles* in Mexico, the most common dried beans used there are, clockwise from top left; **red kidney beans, white kidney beans, lima or butter beans, speckled pinto beans,** and **small black turtle beans.** Purple *flor de mayo* (not shown) are also common. All need presoaking or long cooking. Dried red beans must be boiled briskly for at least 15 minutes at the start of cooking to deactivate toxins.

SUGAR AND CHOCOLATE

4. Chocolate, native to Mexico, and locally produced sugars, from top left:

Piloncillo (top and bottom) is a golden unrefined sugar. If unavailable, brown sugar may be used instead.

Mexican chocolate (right), which commonly also contains cocoa, almonds, sugar, and cinnamon, is often sold in round disks. It should be grated or chopped before use.

Plain or bitter chocolate (center left) may be used instead. Both are used in mole sauces.

FLOURS AND GRAINS

5. Though other grain products are used, those native to the Americas include, from left:

Quinoa, a tiny (like birdseed), yellow pseudo-grain. High in protein it is cooked as is rice but for shorter time (page 73).

Masa harina is a flour ground from lime-treated corn, available as yellow, blue, or white. It is used to make fresh masa (dough) for tortillas, tamales, and breads. In Mexico, it can be bought freshly made and damp, but it is perishable. Other corn-based products such as polenta and cornstarch are not suitable substitutes.

Pozole (right) are dried, lime-treated, husked corn kernels, used in soups and stews. All are available from specialist stores.

PORK CRACKLING

6. Pork crackling (*chicharrón*) is pork rind fried to crisp, airy, crunchy sheets. A similar product is popular in another former Spanish colony, the Philippines. Chicharrones are sold in Latin-American and Asian stores.

Making tortillas

Tortillas, like most unleavened flatbreads, are very easy to make. There are two kinds—corn tortillas made with masa harina flour and tortillas made from all-purpose wheat flour (full recipes are given on pages 22 and 25). The doughs are made in the same way, although the ingredients, listed below, are slightly different. Tortilla presses are sold in specialist kitchen shops but, if unavailable, an Indian chapatti press could be used instead. Alternatively, use the rolling pin method described here.

Ingredients
Corn Tortillas
2 cups instant masa harina flour
½ teaspoon salt
1¼ cups warm water
2–4 tablespoons corn oil (optional)*

Flour Tortillas
2½ cups all-purpose white flour
1 teaspoon salt
5 tablespoons lard or shortening
⅔–¾ cup warm water

* Corn oil is not traditional, but I find it makes the tortillas easier to handle.

Making tortilla dough

1. Mix the instant masa harina flour or all-purpose flour in a bowl with the salt. Rub in the lard or shortening (for flour tortillas only.) Add the warm water and stir with a wooden spoon or knead with your hand to make a firm, putty-like dough. Add the corn oil to the corn tortilla mixture if preferred. Shape the dough into a ball, cover with a damp cloth, and let stand for 5–10 minutes. Divide into 20 small balls.

Making tortillas in a press

2. Slit a clear 6-inch plastic bag along two of its sides and open out flat. Sprinkle with a little flour, put a small ball of dough on one side of the plastic, and flatten it gently with one hand. Fold the plastic over the top and put the whole thing into the tortilla press.

3. Push the press several times until the tortilla is the required size. Remove and reserve in the bag until ready to cook.

Forming tortillas with a rolling pin

4. Put a small ball of dough into a plastic bag prepared as described above.

5. Gently roll out the tortilla with a rolling pin, turning the bag by one turn with each roll until the tortilla is an even circle of the required size. Remove and cook as below.

Cooking tortillas

6. Heat an ungreased, heavy-bottom skillet over moderate heat. Pull off the plastic, put the tortilla on your open hand and transfer to the hot skillet. Cook for 30–45 seconds or until blotchy, blistered, and speckled with brown. Using a spatula, turn over the tortilla and cook the other side for 30–40 seconds more. As they are cooked, wrap them in a cloth, put in a lidded basket, and keep them warm until ready to serve. Alternatively, wrap in foil and put in a low oven, about 300°F, reheat in a steamer, or wrap in plastic film and cook on high in a microwave for a few seconds.

Mexican sauces

salsas mexicanas

Adobo mexicano

There are many regional versions of this authentic Mexican barbecue sauce. Derived from the word *adobar*, "to season or marinate," it is widely used in the Philippines as well as Mexico to give flavor to meat, fish, poultry, and even some vegetables. It also tenderizes, preserves, and colors foods, while the dried chiles give a special smoky fragrance.

4 garlic cloves

3 ancho chiles, cored and seeded

10 guajillo chiles, cored and seeded

½ cinnamon stick, crushed

1 fresh bay leaf, torn into shreds

1 teaspoon allspice berries

1 teaspoon black peppercorns

1 teaspoon cumin seeds

1 teaspoon dried oregano, Mexican if possible

½ teaspoon cloves

2 tablespoons dark brown or piloncillo sugar

2 teaspoons sea salt

½ cup cider vinegar or pineapple vinegar

Toast the garlic and chiles in a dry skillet, pressing down frequently until aromatic and lightly blackened (1–3 minutes). Tear up the chiles and grind, in batches, in an electric spice grinder (or mortar and pestle) with the cinnamon, bay leaf, allspice, peppercorns, cumin, oregano, and cloves. Put in a larger blender, food processor, or mortar and pestle and add the sugar, salt, and vinegar. Grind, process, or pound to a paste. Transfer to a non-reactive container and store in the refrigerator.

Recado rojo *or Recado de achiote*

This brick-red spice paste from the Yucatan is seen all over Mexico. Achiote or annatto is sold in Latin American, Mexican and Spanish delis as a paste, powder, or grains. Keep it in the refrigerator for a handy instant condiment.

2 teaspoons annatto seeds (or ready-made powder or paste)

2 teaspoons sea salt

½ teaspoon allspice berries

½ teaspoon black peppercorns, crushed

2 teaspoons mild chile powder, such as chimayo or molido

½ teaspoon dried oregano, briefly pan-toasted

½ large onion, cut in ½-inch slices

4 garlic cloves, unpeeled

2 tablespoons cider vinegar or other fruity vinegar

5 tablespoons fresh orange juice

2 tablespoons fresh lime juice

Finely grind the annatto and salt in an electric spice-grinder. Add the next 4 ingredients and grind, in bursts, to a powder. Pan-toast the onion and garlic in a very hot, oiled skillet, pressing them down, until soft, aromatic, and browned. Discard the garlic skin. Put the spice mix, onion, garlic, vinegar, and juices in a blender or food processor and work to a paste. Remove, cover, chill, and store in a non-reactive container for up to 4 days.

Salsa roja

This hot, spicy, fruity red-sauce-cum-seasoning is found on Mexican tables as often as we have pepper and salt.

2 slices pineapple, fresh or canned and drained

2 large plum tomatoes, halved lengthwise

2 red bell peppers, halved lengthwise

3 tablespoons fruity olive oil, annatto oil, or corn oil

2 tablespoons dark brown or piloncillo sugar

2 chipotle chiles, with stems and seeds

1 teaspoon hot paprika

a small bunch fresh mint, arugula, or baby spinach, chopped

6 tablespoons pineapple, orange, or lime juice

½ teaspoon salt

Put the first 3 ingredients on a baking tray, brush with half the oil, and sprinkle with sugar. Roast 20–30 minutes at 475°F or broil 6–10 minutes until slightly charred. Seed and skin if preferred. Heat the remaining oil in a pan, add the chiles, and cook for 2–3 seconds each side. Stem, chop, and add to the fruits. Add the paprika, mint, juice, and salt and grind to a coarse salsa in a food processor or a stone mortar and pestle.

Bocaditos (little mouthfuls), *antojitos* (little whims), and *botanas* (little dishes served with drinks)—no matter what they're called, these snacks and appetizers are some of the most delicious in Mexican cuisine and consequently, around the world these are the best-known of all Mexican dishes.

Tacos, fajitas, empanadas, and tamales are the most common, but there are dozens of others from many other regions of the country. They make impromptu party foods,

antojitos y botanas

snacks and appetizers

instant finger foods, splendid snacks, perfect starters, and a large table of these dishes will provide an elegant fiesta-style celebration, especially when served with typical Mexican accompaniments—the salsas, recados, adobos, moles, and dips such as the famous green purée of avocado, guacamole.

Store-bought corn tortillas and flour tortillas can be used to assemble some of these dishes, but you may like to make your own using the two easy recipes in this book.

Make up a selection of these recipes for every day and for partying too. They taste wonderful and are good for you. They're very no-fuss, casual foods for families or singles, perfect as snacks, appetizers, or as light meals in themselves.

All Mexican cooks make great use of local herbs and vegetables, with a touch of chile, spice, and citrus—vary these recipes by using what's in season in your own part of the world.

Above all, be adventurous, as Mexican cooks are!

Plantain crisps are best made by thinly slicing the flesh lengthways using a mandoline or vegetable peeler so they curl into long loops, perfect for dipping into an accompanying salsa. Add more or less of the fresh chile to the sauce, according to taste.

Plátano macho frito

Spiced Plantain Chips *with Mango Salsa*

Margarita
Tequila-Lime Cocktail

juice of 5 limes
3–4 teaspoons salt
2 cups crushed ice or ice cubes
¾ cup white tequila
⅓ cup triple sec or Cointreau
Serves 4–6

Pour the juice of 1 lime into a saucer. Spread the salt in another saucer. Dip the rim of each glass first into the lime juice and then into salt. Let dry while you make the cocktail.

Put the ice, tequila, triple sec, and remaining lime juice into a large blender and run for 30–45 seconds. Pour into the glasses and serve with snacks such as plantain chips.

Variation:
For a stronger, shorter version, shake the ingredients with ice in a cocktail shaker. Strain.
Makes 3-4 short drinks.

2 teaspoons dried pepper flakes
2 teaspoons sea salt flakes
2 teaspoons finely grated orange zest
4 cups peanut or corn oil, for frying
2 green plantains or 3 large green bananas

Mango Salsa:
1 medium-hot red chile, such as fresno, jalapeño or Anaheim, or poblano, roasted, skinned, seeded, and sliced
½–1 serrano chile (red or green), sliced

1 medium mango, peeled, stone removed, and flesh finely diced
½ papaya, peeled, seeded, and diced
1 small red onion, finely diced
juice of 2 limes
juice of 1 orange
2 tablespoons well-seasoned fish stock or light soy sauce
2 garlic cloves, chopped
2 teaspoons superfine sugar

Serves 4 as a snack

Toss the pepper flakes, salt, and orange zest together in a bowl, then heat the oil in a medium saucepan or deep-fryer to 375°F. Peel the plantains and slice into long thin strips using a mandoline or vegetable peeler. Deep-fry in batches in a frying basket until golden and crisp. Remove from the oil and drain on crumpled paper towels. Toss, while still hot, in the chile, salt, and orange mixture.

To make the salsa, either stir the ingredients together in a bowl, or purée very briefly in a food processor or mortar and pestle—the texture should be very coarse. Spoon over the chips or use as a dipping sauce.

Serve the crisps with drinks such as this Margarita or with *pulque*, the cloudy Mexican spirit made from the grey-green maguey cactus.

Guacamole is found on almost every table and street stall in Mexico. It is a mistake to make it too smoothly civilized—leave some texture, but scrape the flesh right down to the skin for maximum, intense green. Try to use *guacamole* within the hour, but to keep its vivid color, brush with citrus juice and press over a layer of plastic film to exclude all air. (Adding the stone will not stop discoloring.)

Guacamole

Spicy Avocado Dip

Mix the scallions, chiles, garlic, and cilantro in a bowl. Cut the avocados in half lengthwise and discard the stones. Using a teaspoon, scrape the flesh away from the skins and mash it well while still in the skin. Add to the bowl, together with the salt and half the lime juice. Mix well, smooth the top of the guacamole, and pour over the remaining juice. Top with the diced tomato and serve with tostadas (tortilla chips) for dipping.

Variations:
Guacamole is also good without tomato, and you can also serve it with chicharrones, the crispy Mexican pork cracklings, instead of tostadas.

6 scallions, finely chopped

1–2 fresh, medium-hot green chiles such as serranos or jalapeños, seeded and chopped

2 garlic cloves, crushed and chopped

a handful of fresh cilantro leaves, chopped

2–3 butter-soft ripe avocados

½ teaspoon salt

juice of 1 lime (about 3–4 tablespoons)

1 large ripe tomato, halved, seeded and diced, or 1 (8 oz.) can tomatillos, drained

Serves 2–4

These easy-to-assemble snacks are named after the colorful boats at Xochimilco. Use homemade corn tortillas or the store-bought ready-made taco shells—which are not Mexican at all, but a Tex-Mex invention. Make the tortillas according to the method on pages 8–9, and you can ring the changes by substituting blue corn masa harina, or cutting the tortillas into segments, then deep-frying at 375°F to make chips (tostadas).

Chalupas de Xochimilco

Tortilla Boats from Xochimilco

Tortillas de maíz
Corn Tortillas

2 cups instant masa harina flour
½ teaspoon salt (optional)
1¼ cups warm water
2–4 tablespoons corn oil (see note)
Makes 20

Following the method on pages 14–15, mix all the ingredients in a bowl and knead to a firm, putty-like dough. Shape into a ball, cover with a damp cloth, and let stand for 5–10 minutes.

Divide into 20 pieces and flatten each piece with the heel of your hand. Press in a tortilla press, or roll with a rolling pin until very thin. Cook in a hot, dry non-stick skillet until brown-spotted and dry on both sides.

Wrap in a cloth to keep them soft and warm until ready to eat.

8 taco shells or corn tortillas (recipe left)
corn oil, for frying
8 fish pieces (fried, barbecued, smoked, or marinated), about 2 oz. each
2 large tomatoes, diced
1 cup refried beans (page 70), or guacamole (page 21)

8 crisp green lettuce leaves, finely sliced
½ cup sour cream or 1 cup crumbled cheese, such as *queso fresco* (page 9) or feta
2 limes, cut in wedges, to serve

Serves 4–8

To make your own taco shells, first fill a saucepan one-third full of oil, or a deep-fryer to the manufacturer's recommended level. Heat the oil to 350°F.

Make a thick sausage of crumpled aluminum foil and wrap a tortilla around the foil in a taco shape. Take the tortilla parcel in long-handled tongs and lower carefully into the hot oil, holding it under the oil until it becomes crisp and golden. Drain on crumpled paper towels and repeat until all the taco shells are made.

To assemble the *chalupas*, fill each taco shell with a portion of the next 4 ingredients, in order, finishing with a drizzle of cream or a sprinkling of crumbled cheese. Serve, topped with a lime wedge for squeezing.

Note: Oil is not a traditional ingredient for corn tortillas, but I find it makes the dough easier to handle.

I first tasted these delectable, slim, rolled tortilla flutes in Mexico City—filled with chicken, salsa, and creamy cheese which trickled deliciously down my sleeve. This version omits the cream but includes herbs. Easy and great for hearty teenage appetites or cut in half and served as a stylish snack to go with drinks. These tortillas are made with wheat flour—useful if masa harina is hard to find—but you can also make them with the corn tortillas on page 22.

Flautas

Tortilla Flutes

6–12 uncooked flour tortillas (recipe right)

8 tablespoons sauce such as Salsa rojo (page 17)

8 oz. cooked chicken, finely sliced

a small bunch of fresh cilantro, chopped

peanut or corn oil, for frying

To serve (optional):

guacamole

sour cream

sprigs of cilantro

12 olives, pitted and halved

Makes 6

If the tortillas are small, overlap them by about 3 inches. If large, use only one. Put a portion of sauce on one edge, then add chicken and cilantro. Roll up the tortillas, leaving the ends open, or tucking them in like envelopes. Secure with string or a toothpick.

Brush the base of a large, heavy-based, preferably non-stick skillet with oil and heat until very hot. Add the flutes, 3 at a time and cook for about 2–3 minutes on each side, or until crisp and golden. Turn over with tongs and crisp the other side. Drain on crumpled paper towels. Remove the toothpicks, if using, and serve hot with your choice of guacamole, sour cream, cilantro, and olives.

Variation:

Alternatively, to serve at a party, cut the *flautas* in half and stack them, open ends upward, in a bowl, basket, or banana leaf wrapping.

Tortillas de trigo
Flour Tortillas

2½ cups all-purpose flour

1 teaspoon salt

5 tablespoons lard or shortening

about ⅔–¾ cup warm water

Makes 20

Make the tortillas according to the method on page 15, rolling the dough into 24 small balls, then pressing or rolling into 5–6-inch disks.

Heat a non-stick or heavy-based skillet to medium hot and cook following the method on page 15. Stack, covered, in a cloth-lined basket to keep them soft and warm until ready to eat.

Alternatively, wrap the cooked tortillas in a damp cloth, then in foil and put in a steamer or low oven. They can also be wrapped then frozen.

Beans of many kinds are staple foods in Mexico, from the ubiquitous black bean, to pinto beans, red kidney beans and the lima beans–also known as butter beans—used here. The patties are delicate to handle so use a spatula (the interior softness is part of the charm.) Cook them in oil if you like, but there's no denying that bacon fat and beans are a union made in heaven!

Tortitas de alubias y papa

Lima Bean and Potato Patties

1½ cups dried lima or butter beans,
    soaked in boiling water for 2 hours
    (or overnight in cold)
a large sprig of thyme
1 lb. floury potatoes (baking-style)
1¼ cups mature cheddar cheese, grated
1 teaspoon dried chile flakes

2 garlic cloves, crushed
1 egg, beaten
1 teaspoon sea salt
dried breadcrumbs or flour, to coat
vegetable oil or bacon fat, for frying

Makes 8, serves 4

Drain the soaked, softened beans. Put in a large saucepan, cover with boiling water, bring to a rapid boil, and cook, uncovered, for 15 minutes. Add extra boiling water and the thyme and part-cover the pan. Cook at a gentle boil for 1½–2 hours until the beans are soft enough to mash easily between the fingers, then drain.

Meanwhile, cook the potatoes in boiling salted water, then drain and mash well. Mix in the beans, then add the cheese, chile flakes, garlic, and egg. Mix and knead to a smooth paste and season to taste.

Spread the breadcrumbs or flour in a shallow dish. Heat the oil in a large, non-stick skillet. Dip 4 patties, one after the other, into the breadcrumbs or flour to coat, then into the hot oil. Sauté for 6 minutes (turning once, carefully, halfway through, using a spatula), until golden and crisp. Wipe or rinse the pan between batches and add more oil if necessary. Serve hot with tomato-based salsa or a pico de gallo (page 66).

Note: Mini *tortitas*, cooked for half the time, are great with cocktails.

1 lb. fresh corn masa harina dough
for tortillas (recipe page 22)

Picadillo Filling:
8 oz. ripe tomatoes, pan-toasted*
3–4 tablespoons fruit juice, such as
citrus, mango, or pineapple
1 tablespoon lard or corn oil
2½ cups lean ground pork
2 garlic cloves, chopped
1 small onion, chopped
1 medium plantain or green banana,
peeled and chopped
½ teaspoon cloves
½ teaspoon peppercorns
½ teaspoon cinnamon stick pieces
½ teaspoon salt
½ cup chopped dry-roasted almonds
or peanuts
⅓ cup seedless raisins or crystallized
fruits such as pineapple, mango, or
peach, chopped
4 tablespoons fruit vinegar, such as
cider vinegar
corn or peanut oil, for frying

Makes 12, serves 4–6 (plus extra filling)

* To pan-toast tomatoes, chiles, or
peppers, remove the skin by charring
in a dry skillet, under a broiler, or
over a barbecue or open gas flame.

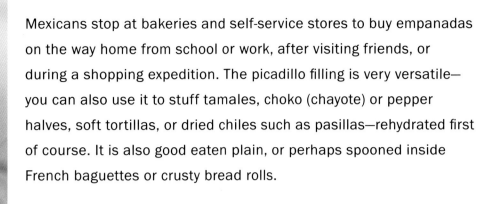

Mexicans stop at bakeries and self-service stores to buy empanadas on the way home from school or work, after visiting friends, or during a shopping expedition. The picadillo filling is very versatile—you can also use it to stuff tamales, choko (chayote) or pepper halves, soft tortillas, or dried chiles such as pasillas—rehydrated first of course. It is also good eaten plain, or perhaps spooned inside French baguettes or crusty bread rolls.

Empanadas de picadillo

Turnovers with Picadillo Filling

To make the empanada dough, make the corn tortilla dough recipe on page 22, then roll it into a ball, wrap it in plastic film, and chill for at least 30 minutes until quite cold.

To make the picadillo filling, put the tomatoes and juice into a blender, food processor, or mortar and pestle and work to a pulp. Heat the lard or oil in a large, heavy-based or non-stick skillet and brown the pork, pressing down and stirring until well-cooked and no longer pink. Stir in the onion and plantain.

Put the cloves, peppercorns, cinnamon, salt, and half the nuts into an electric spice grinder or mortar and pestle and grind to a powder. Add the mixture to the pan, together with the tomato juice and pulp, the remaining chopped nuts, raisins, and vinegar. Stir and simmer, covered, for about 10 minutes until rich, sweet, and reduced.

Divide the tortilla dough into 12 and roll into balls. Press or roll to make tortillas about ⅛ inch thick, as shown on page 14–15.

Weigh out 12 oz. of the picadillo filling mixture and divide into 12 portions—about 1 oz. each. Keep the rest for other uses. Set 1 portion on 1 half of each circle and wet the edges of the pastry. Fold the tortilla in half, excluding the air, and press firmly together. Crimp the edges using your fingers or a fork, or start from one corner and make a wave-and-rope pattern, pressing with your thumb. Repeat with the other tortillas and put on a baking tray.

Heat the oil to 350–375°F in a deep saucepan or deep-fryer. Cook 2–3 at a time (no more) for 2–3 minutes on each side until crisp and golden. Drain on crumpled paper towels. Serve hot, with a salsa, pico de gallo (page 66), or even guacamole (page 21). Serve as a snack or a light meal.

You can also make half-size *empanaditas* to go with elegant cocktails.

This versatile meat filling is used in various ways: wrapped in soft tortillas, in enchiladas or burritos, served in baguettes or crisp white rolls, or as tortas with salad leaves, avocado, and soft cheese. The chipotle chiles used here are the dried form of jalapeños, and can be bought canned or dried (if dried, cover with them with boiling water and simmer for 15–20 minutes). Oregano is usually dry-toasted in a skillet before using in Mexican recipes.

Tinga |

Shredded Beef

1½ lb. beef flank, sliced into strips

8 oz. pork, sliced into strips

juice of 1 lime (optional)

4 fresh bay leaves, bruised

1 teaspoon salt, or to taste

8 oz. chorizo or other spicy sausages, thickly sliced

8 oz. fresh tomatillos, husked, blanched, and chopped, or canned and drained

2 tablespoons tomato purée

4 tomatoes, pan-toasted until dark and soft (page 28), then chopped

½ teaspoon dried thyme

½ teaspoon marjoram, fresh or dried

½ teaspoon fresh oregano, dry-toasted

7 oz. canned chipotle chiles, sliced

Serves 4–6

Put the beef, pork, lime juice (if using), bay leaves, and salt into a flameproof casserole. Add boiling water to cover. Return to a boil, skim, cover, reduce to a low simmer, and cook for 75 minutes or until very tender. Let the meats cool in the stock. When cool, drain and reserve the stock. (Chill, then use both the stock and the fat on top for other recipes.)

Using 2 forks or your fingers, pull the meat apart into long shreds. Return to the pan with a little stock to moisten. Heat a skillet, add the chorizo, and cook until crisp and the fat runs. Add to the meat, together with the tomatillos, tomato purée, tomatoes, thyme, marjoram, and oregano. Simmer for 15 minutes, then add the chipotle chiles and serve in the crisp white rolls shown here, with lettuce, avocado, and soft cheese, or any of the other ways mentioned above.

This dark, spicy soup typifies the cooking of Southern Mexico, the Gulf Coast, and Yucatan. Epazote is the traditional flavoring herb (and regarded as wonderful with beans).Because it is difficult to find outside Mexico, I have used cilantro in this recipe. The beans taste best when cooked from scratch, but if time is short, use canned, drained black beans, or lima, pinto, or red kidney beans. Serve this soup as an entree for lunch or dinner with a green salad and fresh fruit salad to follow. Iced beer is a perfect match.

Sopa de frijol negro

Black Bean Soup

6 tablespoons corn oil

8 scallions, chopped

1 lb. cooked or canned black beans (*frijoles negros*—black haricot beans)

4 garlic cloves, chopped

2 green jalapeño chiles, cored and finely sliced

1 teaspoon ground cumin, pan-toasted

1 teaspoon coriander seeds, pan-toasted

2 tablespoons tomato purée

3 cups hot chicken stock

a small bunch of fresh cilantro

1 tablespoon dark brown sugar

salt and freshly ground black pepper

To serve:

6–8 tablespoons sour cream (optional)

1 corn tortilla, rolled and thinly sliced (optional)

2–3 scallions, sliced

Serves 6–8

Heat half the corn oil in a large, heavy-based saucepan, add half the scallions, and sauté them for about 1–2 minutes.

Drain the beans and put into a food processor with the garlic, chiles, spices, and tomato purée. Process to a coarse paste, then pour into the pan of scallions. Stir over moderate heat for 5 minutes or until bubbling and aromatic. Add the stock, cilantro, and sugar. Return to a boil, reduce the heat, and simmer, partially covered, for 20 minutes.

Ladle half the hot soup into the food processor, blend briefly, pour back into the pan, stir well, and return to a boil. To serve, divide the soup between 6–8 heated soup plates and top with a swirl of sour cream, tortilla strips, and scallions.

Variation:

Crunchy pork cracklings—*chicharrones* (page 13)—are delicious crumbled over the soup.

This is a familiar dish to Mexicans and is served after another soup course, not before. It can be made ahead and reheated or, alternatively, eaten warm like a sort of pasta salad. This kind of soup bubbles up in liquid at the start of cooking, like traditional soup, but then simmers until reduced to a dense and dry state. I have used parsley instead of the difficult-to-find Mexican herb, epazote—though even this can sometimes be found growing wild, when it is known by its common name, "goosefoot".

Sopa seca de fideo

Dry Soup with Pasta

2 tablespoons lard or bacon fat

2 tablespoons corn oil

4 oz. dried vermicelli pasta

1 onion, sliced into rings

3–4 garlic cloves, chopped

1 large bunch flat-leaf parsley or
   epazote, tied in a bundle

2 fresh green jalapeño chiles, held
   together by a toothpick

5 cups chicken stock

4 tablespoons tomato purée

2 tomatoes, diced

To serve:

a small handful of flat-leaf parsley,
   chopped

¼ cup shaved or grated Parmesan or
   crumbled goats' cheese

Serves 4–6

Heat the lard or bacon fat and oil in a large heavy-based saucepan. Add the dry pasta and sauté until golden—do not let it scorch. Using a slotted spoon, remove the pasta and set aside. Add the onion and garlic and sauté until soft and aromatic. Add the parsley or epazote, chiles, stock, tomato purée, and diced tomatoes. Stir well and return to a boil.

Add the pasta, stir, cover, reduce the heat, and simmer gently for 15 minutes. Uncover and simmer for 10–20 minutes longer until almost dry. (The time will depend on the size and depth of your saucepan.) Serve, sprinkled with parsley and cheese.

pescados y mariscos

fish and seafood

Some of the most unforgetable meals discovered by visitors to Mexico include fish and seafood dishes. The natural Mexican bounty of lime juice, chiles, sweet herbs, and a little salt sit marvelously well with fishy treats.

Fresh ceviche—pieces of fish "cooked" by the acid effect of lime juice—are one option. Bowls of rosy, shell-on shrimp, sizzled in spices, tossed in a marinade, then finished with a chile-enhanced relish, are another.

With her shores lapped by the Gulf of Mexico, the Sea of Cortès, the Pacific, and the Caribbean, this Central American country promises many piscatorial possibilities. It isn't unusual, for instance, to see a beach barbecue of skewered snapper, pompano, mackerel, or baby shark.

Sizzling pans full of spicy crabs are commonplace. Tamales wrapped in banana leaves or corn husks, with succulent nuggets of salty sweet fish buried inside, are legendary, while the heart-shaped leaves of *hoja santa*, a traditional Mexican herb, wrapped around pieces of southern-style ember-cooked fish give a haunting flavor.

Inland, dishes may consist of freshwater crayfish, dried shrimp and dried salt cod made into fritters—salt cod is a legacy of the colonial past in many parts of the world, especially the islands of the Caribbean. In addition, as in Spain, fish and seafood feature in paella-style composite dishes of great charm.

A versatile recipe using a Veracruz-style smoky, spicy salsa that flavors the food, while preserving it. Cook the shrimp by sautéeing, as here, or briefly barbecue, broil, or even poach in boiling sea water. Bathe them in this pickle then chill until serving time. *Camarones* are the perfect food for picnics, parties, or fiestas—serve them bathed in sauce and rolled up in soft tortillas.

Camarones en escabeche

Butterflied Shrimp in Chile-Lime Pickle

16–24 large uncooked tiger shrimp,
   in the shell

3 tablespoons corn oil

1 teaspoon sea salt

½ cup fresh lime juice

4 chipotle chiles, with seeds

2 garlic cloves, pan-toasted and
   chopped

1 large tomato, pan-toasted and
   chopped

½ cup fish stock or chicken stock

banana leaf, avocado leaves, corn
   husks, or warm tortillas (optional),
   to serve

Serves 4–6

Slash the outer curve of the shrimp shells and flesh, but leave them joined at the tail. Press down with your palm and flatten—the flesh will spread into a butterfly shape.

Heat a heavy-based skillet, then brush with 2 tablespoons of the oil. Sauté the shrimp, using a spatula to press them onto the skillet until the shells turn pink and the flesh is firm and white. Transfer the shrimp to a large, shallow, non-reactive dish. Sprinkle with the salt and 4 tablespoons lime juice and set aside while you make the pickle.

To make the Chile-Lime Pickle marinade, heat the remaining oil in the same skillet until hot. Add the chiles, and cook for about 8–10 seconds until they become aromatic, slightly brown and puffy, then chop them in a blender. Add the garlic, tomato, remaining lime juice, stock, and a little oil, if preferred. Grind to a smooth salsa. Pour over the shrimp and chill in the refrigerator for 2–48 hours.

Serve on a bed of leaves, or with a pile of warm tortillas.

Note: By lengthening or shortening the cooking time you can adapt this recipe for lobsters, crayfish, or smaller shrimp.

Ceviche is an immigrant dish—it may have come from Polynesia, and is found all over the Pacific and Latin America in one form or another. *Cebar* means "to pierce or penetrate" in Spanish, and that is exactly what the acidity of citrus does: sets or coagulates the protein in raw fish to dense, opaque whiteness so it looks, tastes, and is cooked. No heat is used—just a refrigerator.

Ceviche

Lime-Cured Fish

Slice the fish off its skin in thin diagonal slices, or skin it and cut into ½-inch cubes. Spread over the base of a non-reactive dish, then sprinkle with the lime juice, chiles, and half the onion. Stir a little to ensure the fish is well covered. If necessary add more juice or put into a smaller dish. Chill for 3–8 hours or until the fish is dense, firm, and white all the way through. (Cut a piece to test.)

Strain off the excess liquid and discard the onion. Stir in the tomatoes, oregano, olive oil, and salt and pepper, to taste. Serve with warm tortillas, avocado, the reserved onion slices, and crisp romaine lettuce leaves to use as scoops.

Variation:

Omit the olive oil and oregano and substitute about 6 tablespoons good-quality, thick coconut milk, fresh or canned, and about 2 tablespoons chopped fresh cilantro leaves. This version is also very good with scallops.

1½ lb. very fresh fish fillets, such as red
  mullet, sea bass, mackerel or snapper
1¼ cups fresh lime juice
2 serrano chiles, seeded and sliced
1 white or red onion, finely sliced
  into rings
2 ripe tomatoes, seeded and sliced
2 sprigs fresh oregano or marjoram
2 tablespoons fruity olive oil
salt and freshly ground black pepper

To serve:

warm tortillas
cubed flesh of 1 small avocado (optional)
romaine lettuce leaves

Serves 6–8

Veracruz is famous for its seafood and this is one of Mexico's best-known fish dishes. The recipe works well with snapper, striped bass, or bream, but any dense, white-fleshed fish is acceptable. Cook on top of the stove or in the oven, and allow extra time if using a whole fish. I like this dish served with boiled baby potatoes—the potato is another of those now-commonplace vegetables first imported from the New World (but from the Andes, not Mexico.)

Pescado a la veracruzana

Fish in the Veracruz Style

2 lb. red snapper, bream, or striped bass
    fillets or a 1¾ lb. cleaned whole fish
juice of 1 lemon or 2 limes
4 tablespoons fruity olive oil
4 garlic cloves, chopped
2 onions, sliced into rings
1½ lb. ripe red tomatoes, skinned and cut
    into wedges
¼ cup drained capers or 12 caperberries
½ cup green olives, plain or stuffed

2 canned, drained jalapeño chiles
2 fresh chiles, deseeded and sliced
sea salt and freshly ground black pepper

To serve:
2 lemons or limes, halved or in wedges
canned jalapeño chiles, drained
olives or caperberries

Serves 4

Slash the skin of the fillets or whole fish several times and put into a non-reactive dish. Pour over the lemon or lime juice, rub in salt and pepper, and let stand for 20 minutes.

Meanwhile, heat the oil in a flameproof casserole or skillet large enough to hold the whole fish. Add the garlic and onions and sauté until softened. Add the tomatoes, capers, olives, and chiles, then pour over the fish. Cover and simmer on top of the stove for 8–15 minutes for fillets (longer for whole fish) or until the flesh is firm and white.

Alternatively, cook in a preheated oven at 400°F for about 30 minutes. Serve hot, with lemon or lime wedges, chiles, and olives or caperberries.

Half a millennium ago, the pre-Columbian peoples of Mexico ate a lean, high-fiber diet, which was rich in fish, vegetables, and fruits. Although the ruling classes commonly had some meat available in the form of game—such as rabbit, iguana, armadillo, wild deer, and wild pig, for instance—there were also various indigenous creatures, such as muscovy duck and wild turkey, which had been domesticated.

Chicken, introduced by the Spaniards, later became a major source of sustenance, as did the hog and the goat.

The wild turkey, known as the "double chin cock," which had been domesticated by the Maya, caused a sensation when introduced to Europe's royal courts: it was thought a great improvement on peacock, never the most succulent of birds.

pollo y guajolote

chicken and turkey

Interestingly turkey, which is now so closely associated with North American feasts, was introduced there from Europe.

Today, chicken and turkey feature high on the list of festival favorites and everyday foods. Just a few possibilities include dishes such as tamales, enchiladas with shredded chicken, *pipiàns*—the thick stews of many rainbow colors, thickened with nuts or seeds, and adobos—the spicy treatments used in both quick and slow-cooked poultry dishes.

Mole poblano, made with the totally indigenous ingredients of turkey, chocolate, and chiles, though a marathon effort to prepare, is justly famous as Mexico's national dish.

Tamales are fiesta foods—for parties, family celebrations, and traditional Day of the Dead festivities. This version includes chicken mixed with a delicate green salsa. It is a refreshing and versatile sauce, superb with many *antojitos*, broiled food, barbecued fish and poultry, and many tortilla and cheese-based dishes.

Tamales verdes de pollo

Chicken Tamales with Green Sauce

1 lb. cooked, finely sliced chicken

½ cup salsa verde (see below)

tamale dough (see below)

10 oz. fresh corn husks or 5 oz. dried

Tamale Dough:

½ cup bacon fat, lard, or shortening

3½ cups masa harina flour

1 teaspoon baking powder

2–2¼ cups chicken stock

Salsa Verde:

1 zucchini, sliced

1 lb. fresh tomatillos, quartered or
  1½ lb. canned tomatillos, drained

2–3 fresh jalapeño or serrano chiles,
  seeded and chopped

a handful of fresh cilantro, chopped

2 garlic cloves, crushed

2 tablespoons lard or corn oil

1 cup chicken stock (approximately)

½ teaspoon salt

Makes 16–20

To make the salsa verde, blanch the zucchini and fresh tomatillos, if using, in boiling water, drain, then simmer in a little boiling water until tender. Drain, then mash with a fork. Put into a food processor or mortar and pestle with the chiles, cilantro, and garlic and process to a coarse pulp. Do not over-process. Heat a large, heavy-based skillet, add the lard or oil and pulp. Cook, stirring, over high heat for 5 minutes. Add stock and cook for 5 minutes until thickened again. Cool, season, and refrigerate for up to 3 days.

When ready to make the tamales, mix the chicken with ½ cup of the salsa verde, reserving the rest for serving.

To make the tamale dough, put the bacon fat, lard, or shortening into a food processor or electric mixer and purée about 1 minute until fluffy. Add half the masa harina, half the baking powder, and half the stock. Mix briefly, then mix in the remainder to form a soft, cake-like batter.

To make the tamales, choose the biggest corn husks, about 4 inches wide. If using fresh corn husks, soak briefly in salted cold water. If using dried, cover in hot water, weigh down, and bring to boiling. Simmer 5 minutes, then let stand until cool.

To assemble the tamales, put about 2 tablespoons dough in the center of 1 large husk. Top with 2 tablespoons chicken-salsa filling. Enclose the filling with the 2 side flaps, folded inward and over. Fold over the 2 ends to overlap into a neat parcel. If not secure, wrap again with smaller husks until firm. Secure with toothpicks or string.

When all the tamales are made, put a layer of corn husks in the base of the steamer, add the tamales, stacked vertically, and cook over a steady heat for 1 hour (some recipes recommend 3 hours) or until firm. Do not allow to boil dry—top up with boiling water as needed. When cooked (test by opening one), serve hot with extra salsa verde, pico de gallo (page 66) or other salsa (pages 17, 20).

The adobo spice mixture—from *adobar*, meaning "to season or marinate"—is the great Mexican barbecue sauce. Many versions exist and there are a number of regional differences. Mexicans love it, and it is a truly wonderful flavoring for fish, meat, poultry, game, and even some vegetables. At the same time, it also tenderizes, preserves, colors, and gives the food a special smoky fragrance.

Brochetas de pollo en adobo

Chicken Kebabs in Spicy Marinade

Cut the chicken into 1-inch chunks, then thread it evenly onto 8 bamboo or wooden skewers. Put them in a shallow non-reactive dish and spoon over about ⅔ cup of the adobo until well coated. Refrigerate for at least 15 minutes and up to 1 hour, turning the pieces several times in the marinade.

When ready to cook, drain the kebabs and either discard the marinade or put it in a saucepan, add ½ cup water, boil for several minutes, then serve as an accompaniment.

Cook the kebabs under a preheated broiler or on a barbecue over aromatic wood. Alternatively, roast on an oiled, foil-covered baking tray in a preheated oven at 400°F for 20–25 minutes or until hot, crusty, tender, and aromatic.

Serve with the remaining adobo, together with accompaniments such as soft tortillas, a salsa, and guacamole (page 21).

Note: The wooden skewers should be damp enough after marinating so they won't burn or char when placed on the barbecue or under the broiler, but you may like to soak them in water for 15–20 minutes first to make sure.

4 large chicken breasts or 1½ lb.
  boneless, skinless chicken thighs
1 quantity Adobo mexicano (page 16)

Serves 4

about 6 lb. turkey pieces, plus giblets

a large handful of fresh parsley

4–6 tablespoons lard

8 dried mulato chiles

2 dried ancho chiles

1 dried pasilla chile

2 canned chipotle chiles, drained

2 tablespoons sesame seeds

1 teaspoon coriander seeds

2 tomatoes, chopped

2 oz. Mexican chocolate, or dark,
bitter chocolate, chopped

¼ cup toasted or unblanched almonds

2 tablespoons seedless raisins

2 tablespoons pumpkin seeds

1 onion, sliced

3–4 garlic cloves

2 corn tortillas, torn or crumbled

¼ teaspoon cloves

¼ teaspoon aniseed

¼ teaspoon black peppercorns

½ cinnamon stick, crushed

sugar, to taste

salt and freshly ground black pepper

Serves 8–12

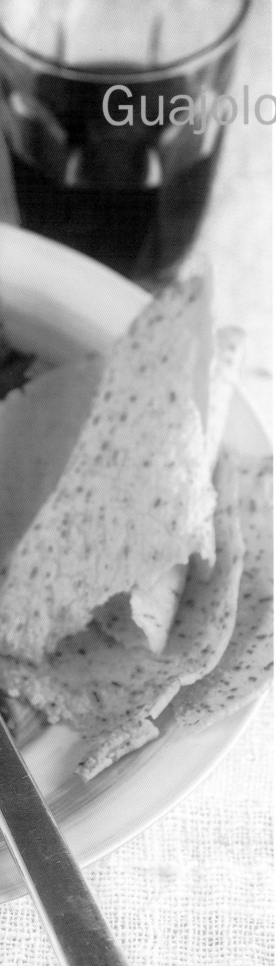

Guajolote en mole poblano

Turkey Mole

To make the turkey stock, put the giblets and parsley into a Dutch oven with 4 cups water. Bring to a boil, skim, cover, and reduce the heat to a simmer. Cook for 45 minutes to 1 hour while you prepare the sauce, then season to taste.

Heat 2 tablespoons lard in a large, shallow, heavy-based skillet and sauté half the turkey pieces for 10 minutes or until golden. Transfer to 1 large or 2 medium roasting pans, cover with foil, and keep them warm in a very low oven while you brown the remaining turkey pieces.

Core and seed the dried chiles then tear into 2-inch pieces. Keep the canned chipotles separate. Dry-toast the dried chile pieces in a hot skillet for 1–2 minutes until aromatic (do not let them scorch). Toast the sesame and coriander seeds in the same pan until golden and aromatic. Cool, reserve some of the sesame seeds for serving, and add the remainder to the chopped tomatoes. Add the chocolate and a little more lard or turkey fat to the hot skillet.

Cover the pieces of toasted dried chile with 3 cups boiling water, weigh down with a plate to keep them submerged, and soak for 30 minutes. Add the chipotle chile.

Heat a little more lard or turkey fat in a skillet and sauté the almonds, raisins, pumpkin seeds, onion, and garlic all together for several minutes. Using a slotted spoon, transfer to the tomato mixture. Sauté the tortilla pieces briefly and add to the mixture.

Transfer, In batches, to a blender or food processor and grind to a smooth sauce with the chiles, cloves, aniseed, peppercorns, and cinnamon, using a ladle of turkey stock each time. (Traditionalists would now sieve this sauce—I do not. Please yourself.)

Add this mixture to the large skillet and cook, stirring, over moderate heat until darkened and thickened—about 3–5 minutes. Add the remaining turkey stock, strained. Simmer for 30 minutes or so until creamy. Season with salt, pepper, and a little sugar, if needed, to taste. Pour this finished sauce all over the browned turkey. Cover with foil or a lid and bake at 350F° for 1½–2 hours. Lift the turkey onto a large serving platter. Stir the sauce left in the pan(s) and pour over the bird. Scatter with the reserved sesame seeds. Serve hot, with tortillas, vegetables, or salad.

Variation:
Some cooks prefer to poach the pieces of turkey in stock while the sauce is prepared. Drain it, quickly brown it, then reheat briefly in its sauce.

borrego, puerco y res

lamb, pork, and beef

Mexican cuisine is justly rated by experts as one of the great five, along with French, Italian, Chinese, and Indian. Nowhere is this more visible than in recipes for lamb, pork, and beef, as well as poultry and game. The Spanish had introduced beef cattle, sheep, and domestic hogs, so Mexicans adapted their recipes for cooking indigenous wild animals to the new ingredients. Many of these recipes include sauces, salsas, recados, *pipiàns*, adobos, moles, and other seed, spice, chile, and herb mixtures as an integral part of the dish.

The range is breathtaking, the flavor complexity startling, the colors and textures mysterious, rich and often ancient in concept. Most are easily achieved using modern tools, a broiler or barbecue, a spice-grinder or food processor, as well as the ancient *molcajete* (basalt mortar and pestle).

Many of these dishes can be deconstructed into simple ways of roasting, braising, broiling, barbecuing, or making tamales with an independent spice or herb dressing-cum-paste component. Serve these meats on their own, or with vegetables, rice, beans, breads, and tortillas. The flexibility is absolutely superb, the possibilities exciting.

Yucatan spice pastes (recados—page 17) are famous. Many include annatto seeds which give a rich, red-gold color and an earthy taste—especially good with barbecued and broiled meats. In this recipe the meat should be uniformly about ¾ inch thick (slash thicker areas) and opened flat in a butterfly shape. Use wood, not briquettes, to fire your barbecue—in Mexico mesquite is preferred for its aroma.

Barbacoa de borrego

Barbecued Butterflied Lamb *with Red Recado*

1 leg of lamb, about 3-4 lb., boned
    and butterflied (pressed out flat)
2 tablespoons fruity olive oil
1 quantity *Recado rojo* (page 17)

Serves 8-10

Rub the lamb all over with the oil. Set on a non-reactive tray or flat dish. Rub the *Recado rojo* all over both sides of the lamb, cover loosely, and chill for 2–12 hours. (No longer, or the salt will draw the juices out of the meat, making it too dry.)

If using a broiler, preheat it until very hot. Set the rack to hold the meat 4–6 inches from the heat: if using a barbecue, let the coals die down to a medium heat.

Put the lamb on the oiled rack. Broil or barbecue slowly for 20–35 minutes or until crusty and dark (a meat thermometer inserted into a thick muscle should register about 176°F.) Using tongs, turn the meat around so it cooks evenly, but turn it over only once, about half way through.

Serve in thick slices with a green herbed salsa such as pico de gallo (page 62) or salsa verde (page 60), a leafy salad (page 63), potatoes (page 67) or beans (page 70–71), and a basket of warm soft corn tortillas.

Note: You can also roast this dish in the oven at 475°F for about 45–50 minutes or until the surface is crisp and brown and the meat well-cooked right through—rare lamb is not a Mexican tradition.

Mexicans serve meatballs in many ways—poached in stock and served in the same liquid as a versatile hearty *caldo* (wet soup)—or drained and eaten as an *antojito* with a chile salsa. Alternatively, they can also be quickly pan-fried (as in this version) and eaten in the fingers, on toothpicks, or rolled up inside soft tortillas with guacamole, a salsa, or other accompaniments.

Albóndigas al perejil

Meatballs with Parsley

Toast the oregano in a dry skillet until aromatic, then mix with the lamb, salt, garlic, parsley, and scallions in a bowl. Dip the tortillas or bread into warm water until sodden, then squeeze dry and mash into the mix. Mix in the egg, then squeeze into a firm mass. Divide into walnut-sized balls, rolling them between your palms.

Heat the oil in a skillet, add the meatballs, and sauté, rolling the pan constantly to avoid sticking. Cook for about 6–7 minutes or until firm and evenly golden brown. Remove with a slotted spoon and keep them hot until all are cooked.

Serve hot in lettuce leaves, drizzled with sour cream, and sprinkled with chopped parsley and sliced chiles. Soft flour tortillas and the peppered Mango salsa (page 20) would be other suitable accompaniments.

Alternatively, serve in any of the ways described in the introduction, or refrigerate the meatballs and eat them later, cold.

Note: These meatballs, if served with rice or pasta and beans followed by leafy greens, will easily serve 4–6 people for lunch or dinner.

2 teaspoons dried oregano

1 lb. twice-minced lamb, a mixture of lamb and beef, or lamb and pork

1 teaspoon salt

2 garlic cloves, chopped

4 tablespoons chopped flat-leaf parsley

4 scallions or 2 shallots, chopped

3 oz. torn stale tortillas or bread

1 egg, lightly beaten

corn or peanut oil, for frying

your choice of lettuce leaves, sour cream, chopped parsley, sliced chiles, soft flour tortillas, and Mango salsa (page 20), to serve

Makes 24–32

Mexican recado verde is a wonderfully fresh seasoning, used as a sauce, tenderizer, marinade, and generally delicious condiment. Typically, it is made to accompany a great variety of dishes. This one is a great party recipe using top-quality fillet of beef, simply seasoned—you can use chile instead of peppercorns, if you prefer—seared, then roasted. Traditionally recado was made with a mortar and pestle, but a food processor does the trick in seconds.

Filete con recado verde
Beef Fillet with Green Sauce

Rub the meat all over with the garlic. Sprinkle a shallow roasting pan with the salt, peppercorns, and sugar and shake until well mixed. Roll the meat in the mixture until well coated. Tie the beef around its width in 3 places with string to help it keep a good shape. Set aside while you make the recado verde.

Put the recado ingredients in a food processor or mortar and pestle and process to a coarse green paste. Do not over-purée. Set aside until ready to serve.

Heat the oil in a heavy-based skillet, add the meat, and cook on all sides for a total of 6 minutes until brown. Transfer to a roasting pan and cook in a preheated oven at 400°F for about 25 minutes (or until a meat thermometer inserted near the center registers 125°F for rare meat. Allow about 5–8 minutes more for medium-rare. Remove from the oven, cover with foil, and set aside in a warm place for 5 minutes to set the meat juices.

Serve the beef thickly sliced, with a large spoonful of recado verde, and accompaniments such as char-grilled plantain or plantain chips (page 20) and a choko salad (page 66) perhaps with some blanched broccoli added.

Other uses for recado verde:
1. Skewer *cabrito* (baby goat), pork fillet, or squid on metal skewers. Char-grill or broil until sizzling, aromatic, and firm, then serve with extra recado.
2. Slash sardines or mackerel fillets, rub with recado, broil, and serve with extra recado.
3. Slash fillets of tuna, swordfish, or salmon and rub in recado. Wrap in a banana leaf and bake or barbecue until aromatic and firm.
4. Barbecue or roast corn cobs, plantains, or sweet potatoes. Serve with recado.

2 lb. whole, well-trimmed beef fillet

6 garlic cloves, crushed to a pulp

1 tablespoon sea salt flakes

2 tablespoons black peppercorns, crushed

1 tablespoon dark brown sugar

2 tablespoons corn, peanut, or olive oil, for frying

Recado Verde:

2-inch strip lime zest, finely sliced

4 scallions, chopped

2 garlic cloves, crushed

2 handfuls fresh cilantro leaves, torn

2 handfuls fresh mint leaves, torn

2 teaspoons coarsely crushed black peppercorns

2 teaspoons sea salt flakes

1 teaspoon allspice berries, crushed

Serves 6–8

Roasted pork is served here in an elegant red mole, without chocolate, but with subtle Spanish and Indian influences. Traditionally the meat would be cut up and braised. In this modern version, prime pork loin is pot-roasted whole in a sauce which, in Mexico, might contain nopales (cactus paddles)—an ingredient that may be hard to find outside its home range. Rice, soft tortillas, char-grilled corn, and an insalata mixta would all be delicious accompaniments for this interestingly spiced meat.

Lomo de puerco coloradito

Pork Loin in Rosy Sauce

3 lb. pork loin, skinned and trimmed

2 tablespoons chile powder, preferably ancho

1 teaspoon salt

4 tablespoons lard or corn oil

Mole Coloradita:

3 ancho chiles, stemmed and seeded

2 guajillo chiles, stemmed and seeded

1 teaspoon black peppercorns

2-inch piece cinnamon stick, crushed

1 teaspoon cumin seeds

2 teaspoons dried oregano

4 garlic cloves

¾ cup hot stock (veal or chicken)

2 tomatoes, pan-toasted and chopped

1 oz. candied fruit, such as peach or mango

½ cup toasted, salted almonds, chopped (or unblanched almonds, pan-toasted)

½ cup toasted sesame seeds

fresh oregano sprigs, to serve (optional)

Serves 6–8

Pat the pork dry with paper towels and rub it all over with chile powder and salt. Heat half the lard or oil in a large flameproof casserole on top of the stove and brown the loin on all surfaces for 2–3 minutes. Cover, then cook in a preheated oven at 350°F for 1–1¼ hours or until a meat thermometer registers 195°F.

Meanwhile, to make the mole, pan-toast the dried ancho and guajillo chiles, peppercorns, cinnamon, cumin, oregano, and garlic in a preheated non-stick skillet for about 2 minutes or until aromatic but not scorched. The garlic will need a little longer so press it down to speed the cooking. Chop the chiles. Put all the toasted ingredients into an electric spice-grinder or mortar and pestle and work to a powdery paste. Transfer to a food processor with about ¼ cup of the hot stock and let stand for 10 minutes. Add the tomatoes and blend briefly to a purée.

Reheat the skillet and add the remaining lard or oil and the purée. Sizzle over medium heat until aromatic and slightly thickened.

Purée the candied fruit, almonds, sesame seeds, and remaining stock in the food processor, then transfer to the skillet, stir, and continue to cook until the sauce is creamy and the tastes well blended. Season to taste, then add 1 tablespoon of water to thin the purée a little, if necessary.

When the pork is cooked, remove it from the oven and let stand in a warm place for about 5 minutes to set the juices. When ready to serve, cut the meat into ½-inch slices and arrange on heated dinner plates. Pour the pan-juices into the hot mole, stir, then pour around the meat. Sprinkle with oregano sprigs, if using. Suitable accompaniments include char-grilled corn (page 60), green salad leaves, and sliced rings of red onion.

Chorizo sausages are intrinsic to Mexican cuisine, and take their name from the choricero chile. They can be bought ready-made, or you can make your own, ordering traditional sausage casings from the butcher, or cook them without casings as patties. Chorizos are broiled, sautéed, barbecued, or baked, then eaten plain or crumbled into egg, tomato, or bean dishes—or in tamales, using the dough mixture on page 44.

Tamales de chorizo

Spicy Pork Sausage Tamales

8 oz. lean pork loin

8 oz. boneless pork shoulder

7 oz. pork back fat, chilled

1 teaspoon coriander seeds

1 teaspoon black peppercorns

¼ teaspoon ground nutmeg

¼ teaspoon ground ginger

2 teaspoons dried oregano

2 teaspoons salt

½ cinnamon stick, crushed

1 teaspoon whole cloves

2 tablespoons hot paprika

6 garlic cloves, crushed

3–4 tablespoons vinegar

1–2 tablespoons tequila

2 yards pork sausage casing (optional)

tamale dough (page 44)

banana leaves or corn husks (page 9)

Makes 8–10 chorizos, 20 tamales

To make the chorizo sausages, cut the pork loin and shoulder into 1-inch cubes, and the back fat into ½-inch cubes, then mix all three together.

Put the coriander seeds, peppercorns, nutmeg, ginger, oregano, salt, cinnamon, cloves, and paprika in mixed batches in a spice grinder or mortar and pestle and grind to a powder. Stir in the garlic, vinegar, and tequila, then mix thoroughly into the meat. Let stand at room temperature, covered, for at least 1–2 hours. Put the meat mixture in small batches into a meat grinder or food processor. Grind or process to a rough paste, but do not overwork. Continue until all the meat mixture has been ground, then stir again. Cover and refrigerate overnight to develop flavor and texture.

When ready to cook, use to fill prepared sausage casings, or divide into 8–10 patties. Cook until firm and browned either over a barbecue or in a non-stick skillet.

To make the tamales, wrap pieces of chorizo with tamale dough in banana leaf sections or corn husks, secure with toothpicks or string, and steam for about 1 hour (some traditional recipes recommend 3 hours!) or until firm and compact right through, then serve. A fruity salsa would be a suitable accompaniment.

Variation:

Add ¼ cup of pine nuts, peanuts, raisins, or almonds to the meat mixture.

If you think that about half a millennium ago Bernal Diaz del Castillo, scribe, wrote, "We stood amazed by the infinity of people and goods" as he and Cortès stood in a marketplace in Tlatelolco, you have some idea of the extent of the plant world of Mexico and the rest of the Americas. Take away tomatoes, corn, beans, squashes, peppers, sweet potatoes, chiles, peanuts, and avocados (not to mention chocolate, vanilla, guavas, papayas, and pineapples) from our shopping-lists and what would we do, as cooks? How dull our menus would be.

verduras y ensaladas

vegetables and salads

This gives an inkling of Mexico's great culinary gift to the world. Vast agricultural systems and civilizations have flourished in Mexico since pre-history. Ingenious ways were found to use flowers as fritters, or sweet potato as pudding, or cactus of different kinds to become mezcal, pulque, and tequila, as well as acitron (candied cactus). Cactus paddles (nopalitos) and fruits (cactus pears or Indian figs) also become salad stuffs, fresh snacks, drinks, and desserts.

Throughout this book, you'll find roasted pastes and purées of seeds, nuts, fruits, and vegetables that enliven many dishes, not just vegetables and salads. Some herbs—epazote, *hierba santa* and *hierbabueno*—are difficult to locate outside Mexico. Use my equivalents but don't expect the identical effect. Most of all be creative: these vegetable and salad dishes are just a start.

Simple but superb—roasted corn cobs are bathed in a selection of typical Mexican sauces. Take your choice from Salsa rojo—a richly-flavored three-fruits sauce with mint, the musky undertone of chipotle chiles and a little citrus—or the lemony-tasting tamarind recado, or the fresh flavor of salsa verde. The cobs can be roasted in the oven, charred under the broiler, or cooked over a barbecue.

Maíz rostizado

Roasted Corn *with Red Salsa*

8 tender corn cobs, with husks and
  silks intact
corn oil, for brushing
4 tablespoons diced sweet butter
  (optional)

To serve:
Salsa rojo (page 17)
Tamarind recado (right)
Salsa verde (right)

Serves 4 or 8

Heat a broiler, stove-top grill pan, or barbecue until very hot. Pull back the husks and silks of the corn cobs and rub or brush the kernels with oil. Broil, pan-grill, or barbecue for about 4–5 minutes on each of 4 sides or until brown, tender, and fragrant, or roast in a preheated oven at 400°F for 20–25 minutes. Serve with salsa rojo (page 17), salsa verde, or Tamarind recado (below). If you feel sinful, add extra butter.

Variations:
Tamarind Recado: Pan-toast or broil 1 halved onion, 6 unpeeled garlic cloves, and 2–3 ripe tomatoes until charred and soft, then pull off the skins.

Heat 1 tablespoon corn oil in a small skillet until very hot, and sauté 3 cored and seeded chipotle chiles for 10–12 seconds until softened and slightly darkened. Quarter, core, and seed 1 red or yellow bell pepper and cook in the same way, then chop and put into a blender with the chiles, oil, and ½ cup boiling water.

Let stand 10–15 minutes to develop the flavors, then add ¾ cup tamarind liquid (from Southeast Asian stores) and 2 teaspoons sea salt, and blend to a rich purée. Store, refrigerated, in a non-reactive container, for up to 2 weeks.

Salsa Verde: Simmer 1 sliced zucchini and 1 lb. fresh (or 1½ lb. canned) tomatillos until tender, then drain. Mash coarsely with a fork, then transfer to a food processor or mortar and pestle. Add 2–3 fresh jalapeño or serrano chiles, seeded and chopped, a handful of fresh cilantro leaves, and 1 crushed garlic clove, and work to a rough green paste (do not over-process). Heat 2 tablespoons lard or corn oil in a large, preheated skilled, add the paste, and cook, stirring, over high heat for 5 minutes.

Add about 1 cup chicken stock to moisten. Cook 5 minutes more until thickened. Cool, season, and serve, or refrigerate up to 1 week.

This classic Mexican dish of chiles stuffed with cheese is very different from the Spanish version using bell peppers. Spicy-hot Anaheim or poblano chiles are egg-coated and fried, rather than baked as in the Spanish version. Since they are delicious (and people eat several at a time), you could use good quality canned whole chiles instead. Otherwise allow a bit of time for the preparation.

Chiles rellenos

Stuffed Chile Fritters

Toast the chiles in a dry skillet, then scrape off the skins. Slit open one side of each chile, seed and core, but do not damage the flesh. Insert a slice of cheese into each chile. Push back into shape then roll in the flour.

Using an electric or rotary beater, beat the egg whites and salt until soft peaks form, then beat in the yolks.

Heat 2 inches of oil in a deep saucepan until very hot, about 350–375°F. Dip the chiles into the egg batter and fry several at a time until crisp and golden. Drain on paper towels and keep them warm in a moderate oven. Serve with accompaniments such as spicy rice (page 72), salsa rojo (page 17) or green salad (page 67).

Note: If using canned peppers, drain and dry them well on paper towels, then proceed as above. Piquillo peppers—red, sweet, and spicy—are a good canned variety to use if Spanish Anaheim or poblano are not available. Sold by good delicatessens and Spanish or Latin-American shops, piquillos are half the size of Anaheims or poblanos, so use twice as many.

12 fresh or canned Anaheim or poblano chiles, drained if canned

12 oz. strong cheese, such as Monterey Jack, cut into 12 slices

1 cup all-purpose flour

3 large eggs, separated

a pinch of salt

peanut or corn oil, for frying

Serves 4–6

Roasted pumpkin has a meaty, rich flavor when cooked dry in the oven using interesting spices, and it always looks crusty and delicious. The best varieties for roasting are the larger ones with grey or blue-green skins—butternut squash and other orange-skinned varieties are less distinctive. This recipe is wonderful served with meat and poultry, with bean dishes, and even mashed to a purée and served as a sauce over pasta or rice dishes.

Calabaza rostizada

Spicy Roasted Pumpkin

2 lb. green or grey-skinned pumpkin,
   seeded, then cut into 8 large pieces,
   preferably triangles, optionally peeled
2 tablespoons corn oil or soft butter
1 teaspoon sea salt

1 teaspoon allspice berries
1 inch cinnamon stick, crushed
1 tablespoon dark brown sugar

Serves 6–8

Put the pieces of pumpkin, cut sides up, on an oiled, foil-covered baking tray. Rub or brush with the oil or dots of butter.

Grind the salt, allspice, and cinnamon to a powder in an electric spice-grinder or mortar and pestle. Add sugar, and briefly grind or pound again. Sprinkle over the pumpkin, then roast in a preheated oven at 425–500°F for 25–30 minutes (depending upon the variety and tenderness of the pumpkin).

Serve immediately—the skin can be eaten, or removed by your guests. The flesh can also be mashed with a fork and served drizzled with a fresh, green herb salsa, then wrapped or rolled in soft tortillas.

Variation:
If strong grey-or-green-skinned pumpkin is unavailable and butternut squash is the only alternative, cook as for pumpkin but cut into rounds 4 inches thick.

This is a well-loved Mexican vegetable dish, often served with broiled or barbecued meat dishes. It is also delicious inside soft or crisp-cooked tortillas with garnishes of your choice. The poblanos can be green (unripe) or red (ripe). Ordinary bell peppers are a poor substitute—I would always prefer canned chiles, such as piquillos.

Rajas con crema

Chile Strips in Cream Sauce

6 fresh poblano chiles, roasted, peeled,
and seeded, or 10 oz. canned piquillos,
drained and seeded
4 tablespoons corn, peanut, or olive oil
2 red onions, sliced through the root
into segments
2 garlic cloves, crushed

½ teaspoon salt
½ cup double cream or crème fraîche
the green leaves from 1 scallion
(optional)
tortillas, to serve (optional)

Serves 4

Cut the chiles into ½-inch strips and pat them dry on paper towels. Heat the oil in a heatproof sauté pan or cazuela, sauté the onions and garlic for 3–4 minutes, then add the salt and cream. Stir until the sauce bubbles and is smoothly blended.

Add the prepared strips of poblano, shaking the pan rather than stirring it to avoid breaking the chiles. Heat through, then chop the green scallion leaves, if using, over the dish and serve hot. Tortillas would be a suitable accompaniment.

Variations:

1. Add crumbled soft, salty, white cheese to the rajas and serve in a soft tortilla.
2. Fill a crisp taco shell with finely sliced tender-cooked beef (page 30), pork, chicken, or game, then add the rajas.
3. Top with diced tomato and sliced raw onion.

Papas con chile y ajo

Potatoes with Chile and Garlic

Baby potatoes bathed with garlic, two types of chiles, and a splash of acidity: delicious and very Mexican. Avoid scorching the garlic— it will turn bitter. The type of oil and vinegar is up to you—in Mexico many kinds of mild fruit vinegars are available.

2 lb. small potatoes, walnut-sized or smaller, unpeeled

1 dried guajillo, pasilla, or ancho chile, stem on

1 fresh red poblano chile or red bell pepper, cored, halved, and opened flat

4 tablespoons salted butter

2 tablespoons olive, corn, or annatto oil

8–10 garlic cloves, chopped

1 teaspoon sea salt (to taste)

2–3 tablespoons fruit vinegar, such as cider, red fruits, or pineapple

½ teaspoon store-bought hot pepper sauce (optional)

Serves 4–8

Cook the potatoes in boiling salted water for 20–25 minutes or until tender, then drain. Meanwhile, heat a heavy-based cast-iron or non-stick skillet until very hot. Add the dried chile and press down briefly with tongs or a spatula until the chile is puffy and aromatic. Core and seed, then chop the flesh.

Put the fresh chile or pepper, skin side down, into the same hot skillet. Press down for about 5–10 minutes or until softened, and aromatic. Turn and briefly cook the other side. Chop the flesh finely, skin included. Heat the butter and oil in the skillet, add the potatoes, and sauté for 5 minutes. Add the garlic, sauté for 1–2 minutes, then stir in the salt, vinegar, guajillo, and poblano, and the pepper sauce (if using). Serve hot.

Note: Eaten warm, cool, or cold, these make a great salad served on crisp leaves, with tortillas for wrapping and perhaps a drizzle of yogurt or a crumble of soft cheese.

Ensalada de chayote

Choko Salad *with Avocado*

Choko—found on market stalls in Mexico, South America, and other tropical countries—is also known as chayote, chowchow, christophene, vegetable pear, pear squash, or mirliton. Avocado-shaped, it is a succulent apple-green vegetable of the squash family, and tastes a little like zucchini—which you can use instead, if choko proves difficult to find. In this recipe choko is briefly simmered, then mixed with lime, avocado, and one of Mexico's best-known sauces (and one of my favorites), the colorful raw salsa, pico de gallo—"the rooster's beak".

2 chokos (chayotes)
1 ripe Haas avocado
juice of 1 lime

Pico de Gallo:
2–3 jalapeño chiles, stemmed
   (but not seeded) and finely
   diced

1 large red tomato, finely diced
1 white onion, finely diced
a handful of fresh cilantro, torn
½ teaspoon sea salt
4 tablespoons chicken or
   vegetable stock

Serves 4–6

Peel the chokos if the skin is tough: if not, just wash well. Halve lengthwise, reserve the seed, then slice each half lengthwise into 4–6 pieces. Simmer in boiling salted water for about 10–12 minutes or until tender and soft. Drain and arrange in a dish. (Cook the seed too—it's the cook's treat!)

Meanwhile scoop out the avocado flesh with a teaspoon, add it to the choko, and drizzle with lime juice.

To make the pico de gallo, mix all the ingredients in a food processor or mortar and pestle very briefly (no more than 4 seconds in a food processor), to make a coarse-textured mixture. Spoon over the salad and serve the rest separately. This salsa will keep in the refrigerator for about 3–4 days. It is a useful condiment—almost addictively delicious.

Green salads, with any number of delicious leaves and dressings, are much enjoyed in Mexico. (Caesar salad, perhaps the greatest salad of all, was invented in Tijuana.) Select a balanced mix of ingredients, depending upon what is seasonal and available. If pumpkin seed oil —dark, almost smoky—is unavailable, use half the volume of dark sesame oil, or omit altogether.

Ensalada mixta

Mixed Green Salad

Your choice of:

8 oz. broccoli florets

8 oz. green beans, halved

8 oz. Swiss chard, (green part only) chopped

8 oz. cactus paddles (nopales), fresh or canned and drained, or sliced cucumber

8 oz. baby spinach leaves or purslane (verdolago)

1 large or 2 small crisp lettuces, such as romaine or Little Gem

Pumpkin Seed Dressing:

2 garlic cloves, crushed

a small handful of fresh parsley

a small handful of fresh cilantro

3 tablespoons fresh lime juice

8 tablespoons fruity olive oil

1 tablespoon pumpkin seed oil, or 1½ teaspoons dark sesame seed oil

1 tablespoon brown sugar

Serves 4–6

Put your choice of broccoli, green beans or Swiss chard into a saucepan. Add half their volume of water or stock.

If using fresh cactus paddles, peel, cut the flesh into ½-inch cubes, then add to the other vegetables. Bring to a boil and cook until tender. Drain in a colander, refresh in cold water, then drain again. If using canned cactus, drain, dice into ½-inch cubes and add at this point, or add the cucumber.

Put all the dressing ingredients in a blender and purée. Put the cooked and raw vegetables in a salad bowl, pour over the dressing, toss, and serve.

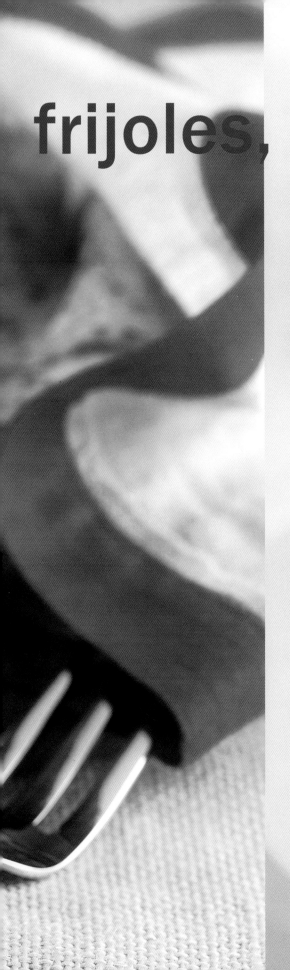

frijoles, arroz y quinoa

beans, rice, and quinoa

Beans, together with corn and chiles, form one of the great anchors of the Mexican kitchen. Their diversity must be seen to be believed: they appear in all the colors of the rainbow, and are used in myriad ways—as purées, pastes, soups, stews, as a vegetable dish in their own right, and as filling or extender for many tortilla-based dishes. Sometimes they are available fresh or newly podded, but more often they are sold dry and must be soaked before use. Almost all the beans used in cooking—except the fava bean and a few others—came from the Americas. They are now so much part of so many cuisines that we forget how recently they arrived, and it is difficult to think of life without them.

Corn, from ancient times, was the staple grain of the Americas, but nowadays others, both native and imported, are also used. Quinoa—pronounced "keen-wah"—is native to Peru and was the staple grain of the Incas. It is now becoming more widely available in healthfood shops and larger supermarkets. In its basic form as grain, it is prepared like rice, making a flavorful risotto (page 73). It is also ground into flour, and can be used to make pasta.

Rice was introduced by the Spanish, adding a further dimension to vegetable cooking. As well as appearing with quinoa, it is also cooked alone (page 73), or in dishes like the soup or *sopa seca* (page 34).

Beans are a great Mexican staple and the type varies according to local tradition. Beans such as black turtles, whites, pintos, limas, pinquitos and reds can all be used in these recipes. Boil for 15 minutes at the start of cooking time: essential to deactivate the dangerous toxins which some dried beans contain. Always top up with boiling, not cold, water. (A slow cooker is not a safe way to cook beans.) The second recipe, for "refried" beans is traditional but not well named—the beans are twice-cooked rather than twice-fried.

Frijoles y frijoles refritos

Beans and Refried Beans

1½ cups dried beans, such as turtle
   beans, kidney beans (see recipe
   introduction), pintos, or pinquitos
2 onions, chopped
8 garlic cloves, crushed
2 fresh bay leaves, crushed
   (or epazote, if available)
2 fresh serrano or other medium-hot
   chiles, crushed but whole
2 tablespoons lard or olive oil, plus
   extra for frying
1 tomato, diced
salt and freshly ground black pepper

Serves 4–6

Wash and pick over the beans, discarding any foreign objects. If there is time, soak in hot water overnight. If not, put in a saucepan, pour over boiling water, and cook at a rolling boil for about 15 minutes, uncovered. Drain, rinse, and drain again.

Put the soaked or semi-cooked beans back into the pan. Add 1 onion, the garlic, bay leaf, and chiles. Cover with boiling water again. Return to a boil, skim off the scum, reduce to a simmer, cover, and cook for 1–1¾ hours or until almost done. Add half the lard or oil, then the salt and pepper. Cook for 30 minutes, then turn off the heat.

Heat the remaining lard or oil in a skillet and sauté the second onion and the tomato. Ladle about 1 cup of beans with an equal amount of the cooking liquid into the skillet. Mash well with a fork to a creamy paste. Drain the remaining beans. Mix this paste back into the beans to thicken the dish. Serve as is, or make refritos (see below).

Refritos ("Refried" Beans):

Heat ½ cup olive oil or 4 tablespoons lard in a skillet. Add 1 ladle at a time of the prepared beans (as above), mashing and heating to a creamy paste, scraping in the crispy browned crust. Continue this process until you have a dryish purée, which will hold its shape, almost like an omelet. Turn it out and use as a filling for enchiladas (tortillas soaked in chile sauce), topped with crumbled cheese, chopped herbs, and sliced red onions as illustrated in the photograph on page 68.

Refritos can be served hot or cold in other ways: in fajitas, tacos, chalupas, or nachitos; with totopos (tortilla crisps), with eggs, salsa, or meats from the broiler.

This excellent bean purée is very flavorful and is a good source of protein. The finely sliced pasilla chiles on top are much less usual than ancho chiles, but they taste very good indeed. Serve this purée as an all-purpose accompaniment for vegetarian foods, meat, or chicken, spooned inside soft tortillas, as a snack, or as a dip.

Frijoles con crema

Creamy Pinto Beans

Soak the beans in a large saucepan of boiling water (discarding any that float) for 2 hours or overnight. Drain, add the onion and boiling water to cover the beans by at least 4 inches. Boil for 15 minutes. Reduce the heat, add the oil, and partly cover the pan with a lid, then cook at a gentle simmer for about 20 minutes or so until tender.

Meanwhile soak the pasilla chiles in near-boiling water to cover, weighing them down. Leave for about 15 minutes. Drain, then cut into rajas (strips).

Drain the cooked beans, reserving about 1 cup of the cooking liquid. Put the onion and about a quarter of the beans into a food processor. Add about a third of the sour cream and a third of the grated cheese. Blend briefly until creamy. Repeat with the next 2 portions. Add a little cooking water to the last portion, then blend leaving quite coarse.

To serve, mix the batches together, spoon into a heated serving dish, and sprinkle the chile strips and crumbled cheese over the top. Add the cilantro, either chopped or in a bunch, and serve the beans while still hot and creamy. Soft corn or wheat flour tortillas or totopos (tortilla crisps) make delicious accompaniments.

2½ cups dried pinto beans

1 onion, halved

2 tablespoons corn oil

3 dried pasilla chiles, slit and seeded

⅔ cup sour cream or crème fraîche

1 cup *queso manchego* or mature Monterey Jack cheese, grated

To serve:

¼ cup *queso fresco* or feta cheese, crumbled

a handful of fresh cilantro leaves

Serves 6

Arroz a la mexicana

Mexican Rice *with Jalapeño Chiles*

This dish is a little like an Italian risotto and can be seen as a kind of *sopa seca* or "dry soup". Traditionally, it was served as a course on its own, though these days it may feature as one of several accompaniments for a main dish of meat, poultry, fish, or game, in much the same way as western cuisines use rice. Serve it as a light lunch or dinner dish in its own right with perhaps a leafy salad to follow. Traditionally, Mexican cooks briefly soak their rice before cooking, so follow the method given here for an authentic effect.

1¾ cups long grain white rice

4 pan-toasted tomatoes (page 25), seeded and chopped

2 tablespoons corn, peanut, or olive oil

1 onion, sliced

4 garlic cloves, chopped

3 cups boiling stock

2 carrots, sliced or diced

2–3 fresh chiles, such as jalapeño, serrano, or fresno

½ cup shelled green peas, fresh or frozen, or 2 oz. baby courgettes, baby asparagus, green beans or yard-long beans, cut in pea-sized dice

Serves 4

Soak the rice for 5 minutes in hot water, swishing it around a little with your hands. Rinse and drain well in a sieve. Meanwhile, put the tomatoes in a blender, food processor, or mortar and pestle and work to a pulp. Purists would strain it, but I leave it as is.

Heat the oil in a heavy-based skillet and sauté the onion and garlic for several minutes. Stir in the rice, sauté for about 2 minutes to coat the grains and begin their cooking. Add the tomatoes, stock, carrots, and chiles. Bring the mixture to a boil, cover, reduce the heat to very low, and simmer for 5 minutes. Uncover, then stir in the peas or other diced green vegetables.

Replace the lid and cook for another 7–8 minutes, undisturbed, until the rice is tender and all liquid is absorbed. Serve hot.

Quinoa is a tiny pseudo-grain which was prized by the original inhabitants of Peru and so precious that it was offered as a tribute to the Inca rulers. Its nutritional profile is high, especially in proteins, and it contains a larger number of useful amino acids than most grains. This green risotto is simple, balanced, and delicious. You can use various kinds of rice, but the type common in Mexico is a slightly fatter version of long grain, which gives a satisfyingly sticky result. Quinoa, also known as amaranth, is sold in healthfood shops, and looks rather like birdseed. The green leafy variety of amaranth sold in Oriental greengrocers should not be confused with quinoa.

Quinoa con arroz

Quinoa Risotto

½ cup quinoa (amaranth)

2 scallions, chopped

1 onion, diced

1 green bell pepper or green poblano chile, cored, seeded, and chopped

4 garlic cloves, chopped

a handful of fresh flat-leaf parsley, torn

a handful of fresh cilantro, torn

2 tablespoons lard, bacon fat, or corn oil

1¼ cups long grain white rice or Italian risotto-style rice

2½ cups boiling chicken or vegetable stock

fresh herbs, to serve (optional)

Serves 4

Blanch the quinoa in boiling water, then drain. Put the next 6 ingredients into a food processor or mortar and pestle and work to a green paste. Heat the lard, fat, or oil in a heavy-based pan or skillet, add half the green mixture, and stir over moderate heat for about 5 minutes. Stir in the rice and blanched quinoa.

Add boiling stock, return to a boil, cover, reduce the heat to very low, and simmer for 15 minutes. (If using the shorter, plumper rice grains, cook for a further 5 minutes.)

Turn off the heat, stir in the remaining green salsa, cover the pan with cloth, and set aside for 5–10 minutes more. Stir, then serve with a small bunch of herbs, if using.

Desserts and sweet foods in Mexico often have great allure. The raw materials, true, are extraordinarily superb but it is the combination of luscious fruits, spices, chocolate and vanilla from the New World, cooked with classic European complexity that gives such vitality.

Spain contributed many recipes to traditional Mexican cooking, and its desserts and custards based on sugar and egg yolk were particularly well received.

postres y bebidas

sweet things and drinks

The country's culinary repertoire was greatly influenced by Empress Carlota—wife of Maximilian, the Austrian Archduke whom Napoleon III of France created Emperor of Mexico. Her Hungarian chef, Tudor, with his team of helpers, marvelously enriched local cooking, especially sweet things such as fine pastries, rich tarts, and tiny cookies. This they managed to do in just three short years, from 1864–67, when Maximilian was deposed by a Mexican army under Juarez.

Richly yeasted breads, doughs, batters, and cakes first appeared on the tables of the rich, while in the country peasants also had a passion for sweet and sticky pastes for fiestas and religious feast days.

Sweetmeats are a basic necessity of life for this sweet-toothed nation—this chapter contains just a taste.

This traditional Spanish pudding, with its glorious, caramelized glossy, sweet glaze topping, is a firm favorite in Mexico. You should aim for a perfect, silky, unblemished, bubble-free texture. To save time, some cooks use half the quantities of canned evaporated milk rather than boiling down 4 cups of whole milk. The flan is then firmer and less silky, but it still tastes deliciously of caramel.

Flan |

Caramel Custard

1¼ cups superfine sugar

vegetable oil, for brushing the sides
    of the tart pan

2 cups evaporated milk

1 vanilla bean, slit lengthwise, or
    1–2 teaspoons vanilla extract

a pinch of salt

4 large eggs

3 large egg yolks

1 tablespoon cornstarch

Serves 6–8

Heat a roasting pan on the middle shelf of the oven at 350°F. Heat a large, heavy-based skillet on the stove, add ½ cup plus 3 tablespoons of the sugar, and swirl the skillet over the heat, without stirring, for about 6–9 minutes or until a deep glossy caramel forms. Lightly brush a 5-cup metal mold (or 6–8 dariole molds, about ⅔–¾ cup each) with the oil, then pour in the caramel mixture.

Pour the evaporated milk into a large saucepan, add the vanilla bean and salt, and bring to a boil. Scrape the vanilla seeds into the liquid. Add the remaining sugar, bring to a boil, uncovered, then cover the pan and set aside.

Beat the salt, eggs, egg yolks, cornstarch, and 1 tablespoon cold water in a large bowl —do not allow it to become too frothy. Pour in the hot milk, stirring. (If adding liquid vanilla, add it now). Strain this custard into the mold or molds, over the caramel base. Set the flan in the roasting pan and pour in enough boiling water to come halfway up the side. Bake, uncovered, for 25–30 minutes or until set. (A knife blade, inserted into the center should emerge clean.) If cooking smaller individual flans, cook for 12–15 minutes.

Lift the flan or flans from the water bath and set in ice water to cool or let cool slowly (about 30–60 minutes). To serve, run a clean knife around the edge of the flan dish. Hold a serving plate over the dish. Invert, sharply, then serve with crisp cookies or cream.

Variations:
1. Add 3 oz. grated unsweetened chocolate to the hot custard, using 5 tablespoons or less of milk. Serve dusted with a mixture of cocoa and confectioners sugar.
2. Substitute 1 tablespoon orange liqueur for the vanilla. Sprinkle with 1 tablespoon finely grated orange zest before serving.

I first tasted this tropical, sweet-scented mango tart in a beach hut café on Mexico's Pacific coast, served with a traditional Mexican delicacy, *cajeta*—a long-cooked (but easy) caramel mixture of goat milk and sugar. Goat milk, happily, is now easier to find in health food shops or larger supermarkets, but if you can't find it whole milk could also be substituted.

Tarta de mango con cajeta

Mango Tart with Caramel Sauce

To make the tart, roll out the pastry and use to line an 8-inch loose-bottom tart pan. Pinch the edges into scallop shapes. Prick the base, line with foil, and put a smaller heavy plate into the pan. Bake in a preheated oven at 425°F for 15 minutes. Remove the foil and plate, bake for 10 minutes more, then remove from the oven.

Fill the tart with mango chunks, standing them vertically. In an electric spice-grinder, work the vanilla bean and sugar to a powder. Scatter this powder and the brown sugar over the fruit. Bake at the top of the oven for 30–35 minutes until the edges of the fruit are crisp. Drizzle with the lime juice, dust with confectioners sugar, and serve hot or warm with *cajeta* (see below), and ice cream or crème fraîche.

Note: *Cajeta* is a traditional accompaniment. Two hours before serving, put 4 cups goat milk, 1 cup plus 2 tablespoons sugar, 1 tablespoon corn syrup and 1 crushed cinnamon stick in a large pan. Simmer and stir in ¼ teaspoon baking soda and 1 teaspoon cornstarch dissolved in 2 tablespoons water (note: it will froth immediately). Increase the heat and cook, stirring occasionally, for 50–55 minutes until thick and dark brown. Cool over ice then serve with the tart. A time-saving tip: short-cut chefs simmer a can (unpunctured) of sweetened condensed milk for 2 hours, let cool, then serve as before.

8 oz. ready-made sweet shortcrust
   pastry, pâte sucrée, or puff pastry
2–3 ripe mangoes, peeled, stoned, cut
   into ½-inch pieces or chunks
½ vanilla bean, chopped
4 tablespoons sugar
2 tablespoons dark brown sugar
juice of 1 lime

To serve (optional):
confectioners sugar, for dusting
cajeta (see left)
ice cream or crème fraîche

Serves 4–6

These light, crumbly cookies (*polvo* is Mexican for "dust") achieve this texture because they are made with lard which, interestingly, contains fewer saturated fats than butter. The powdery effect is enhanced with a thick dusting of sifted confectioners sugar. Though unorthodox, the food processor makes this recipe very easy indeed.

Polvorones

Orange Heart Cookies

Café de olla
Spicy Coffee

1 cup water
8-inch cinnamon stick, crushed
4-inch strip orange zest
1 teaspoon cloves
1–2 tablespoons dark brown sugar
4 cups fresh hot coffee, such as
  Viennese roast, preferably made
  in a cafetière
Serves 6–8

Boil the first 4 ingredients, uncovered, for 5 minutes. Add the sugar and boil for a further 5 minutes.

Pour the coffee and the unstrained syrup into a large heatproof coffee pot or pitcher and serve immediately.

1 cup plus 2 tablespoons lard (see note below), at room temperature
½ teaspoon salt
⅔ cup superfine sugar
3 medium egg yolks
finely sliced zest of 1 orange
finely sliced zest of 1 small lemon

⅓ cup freshly squeezed orange juice
1 teaspoon orange flower water
2 cups white self-rising flour
1⅓ cups white all-purpose flour
confectioners sugar, for dusting

Makes 32–36

Cut the lard into chunks and put into a food processor. Add salt and blend for 1 minute without stopping until the mixture is frothy and light. With the machine running, gradually add the sugar (about 30 seconds). Blend another 30 seconds then, with the motor running, add, one after the other, the egg yolks, zests, orange juice, and orange flower water. Add the flours and blend briefly.

Put the dough on a floured surface, pat out flat, then roll to about ½ inch thick. Cut out shapes using a 2-inch heart cutter or 2-inch diameter circle. Using a spatula, lift onto 2 baking trays. Bake in the middle of a preheated oven at 400°F for 20–25 minutes until golden, with a deeper tinge of brown around the edges.

Transfer to wire racks, dust heavily with confectioners sugar, let cool, then serve with Spicy Coffee. *Polvorones* may be stored in an airtight container for up to 1 week.

Note: If lard is unavailable or unappealing, you may use butter instead, but I would recommend trying this rather old-fashioned ingredient—the effect is delicious.

Index